Step into Science

What's Going On?

Collecting and Recording Your Data

Kylie Burns

Science education consultant: Suzy Gazlay

Crabtree Publishing Company

www.crabtreebooks.com

Crabtree Publishing Company

www.crabtreebooks.com

Author: Kylie Burns
Series editor: Vashti Gwynn
Editorial director: Paul Humphrey
Editor: Adrianna Morganelli
Proofreader: Reagan Miller
Production coordinator: Katherine Berti
Prepress technician: Katherine Berti
Project manager: Kathy Middleton
Illustration: Stefan Chabluk and Stuart Harrison
Photography: Chris Fairclough
Design: sprout.uk.com
Photo research: Vashti Gwynn

Produced for Crabtree Publishing Company by Discovery Books.

Thanks to models Ottilie and Sorcha Austin-Baker, Dan Brice-Bateman, Matthew Morris, and Amrit and Tara Shoker.

Photographs:
Corbis: Jim Reed: p. 4 (bottom left), 25; Papilio: Eric Gilbert: p. 6; Owen Franken: p. 11 (bottom); Sygma: Philippe Giraud: p. 16 (left); Steve Kaufman: p. 27
Discovery Photo Library: Chris Fairclough: p 28
Getty Images: National Geographic: Michael Nichols: p. 7; Sean Justice: p. 9 (center); SuperStock: p. 24 (left); Image Source: p. 26
NASA: JPL Archives: p. 13 (right); NASA, ESA, and the Hubble SM4 ERO Team: p. 18 (left); p. 25 (left)
Samara Parent: back cover, p. 1 (top)
Science Photo Library: Aguasonic Acoustics: p. 21
Shutterstock: cover, p. 1, 3, 9 (top right), 10 (bottom), 20 (left), 25 (right); Anetta: p. 8; Ivanova Inga: p. 10 (top); Oddphoto: p. 11 (top); Chee-Onn Leong: p. 12; Harald Høiland Tjøstheim: p. 20 (right)

Library and Archives Canada Cataloguing in Publication

Burns, Kylie
    What's going on? Collecting and recording your data / Kylie Burns.

(Step into science)
Includes index.
ISBN 978-0-7787-5155-7 (bound).--ISBN 978-0-7787-5170-0 (pbk.)

    1. Science--Methodology--Juvenile literature. 2. Science--Experiments--Juvenile literature. I. Title. II. Series: Step into science (St. Catharines, Ont.)

Q175.2.B435 2010   j507.8   C2009-906461-8

Library of Congress Cataloging-in-Publication Data

Burns, Kylie.
    What's going on? Collecting and recording your data / Kylie Burns.
        p. cm. -- (Step into science)
    Includes index.
    ISBN 978-0-7787-5155-7 (reinforced lib. bdg. : alk. paper)
-- ISBN 978-0-7787-5170-0 (pbk. : alk. paper)
    1. Science--Methodology--Juvenile literature. I. Title. II. Series.

    Q175.2.B427 2010
    507.8--dc22

                    2009044173

Crabtree Publishing Company

www.crabtreebooks.com   1-800-387-7650

Printed in the U.S.A./122009/CG20091120

Published in Canada
Crabtree Publishing
616 Welland Ave.
St. Catharines, Ontario
L2M 5V6

Published in the United States
Crabtree Publishing
PMB 59051
350 Fifth Avenue, 59th Floor
New York, New York 10118

Published in the United Kingdom
Crabtree Publishing
Maritime House
Basin Road North, Hove
BN41 1WR

Published in Australia
Crabtree Publishing
386 Mt. Alexander Rd.
Ascot Vale (Melbourne)
VIC 3032

CONTENTS

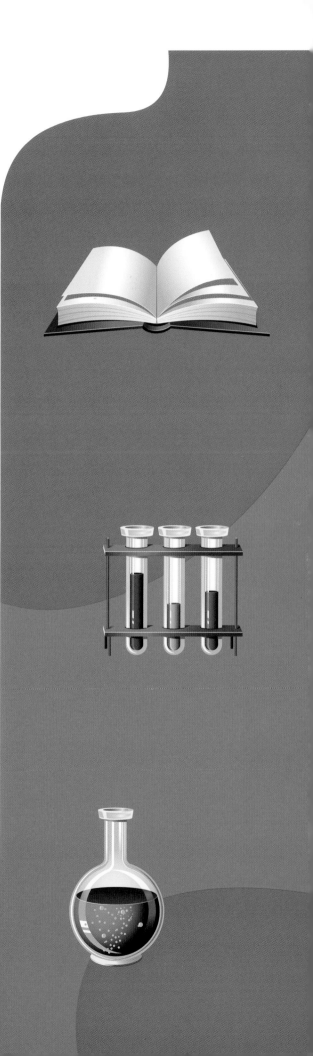

THE SCIENTIFIC METHOD

Have you ever been in an elevator? The **scientific method** is like an elevator—you enter at the first floor and take the elevator up. The elevator passes one floor at a time, and you get closer and closer to your final stop. Sometimes, however, the journey takes you back down before you continue on to reach your destination.

In the same way, following each step in the scientific method is important for making scientific discoveries. Sometimes, though, scientists have to stop, go back, and think again before they continue.

Sharpen your pencils! In this book you will learn how scientists observe their experiments. This is how they get their data. You will also find out how to record data in different ways, including journals, charts, and diagrams.

◄ Collecting data during a tornado is a dangerous job!

Beginning Your Scientific Investigation

Be curious! Questions can come from anywhere, anytime. Questions help scientists make **observations** and do **research**. Science is all about problem-solving!

Making Your Hypothesis

So, what's next? You have a question, and you have done some research. You think you know what will happen when you perform your experiment. The term **hypothesis** means educated guess. So, make a guess and get started!

Designing Your Experiment

How are you going to test your hypothesis? Designing a safe, accurate experiment will give **results** that answer your question.

Collecting and Recording Your Data

During an experiment, scientists make careful observations and record exactly what happens.

Displaying and Understanding Results

Now your **data** can be organized into **graphs**, **charts**, and diagrams. These help you read the information, think about it, and figure out what it means.

Making Conclusions and Answering the Question

So, what did you learn during your experiment? Did your data prove your hypothesis? Scientists share their results so other scientists can try out the experiment, or use the results to try another experiment.

DATA DETAILS

So you've started your experiment, and things are happening! What do you do now?

During an experiment scientists make observations and write down what they notice. This is called recording data. Scientists record data to find out if a hypothesis is true or not. They look at their data closely and look for **patterns**.

The word "pattern" might make you think of your grandmother's wallpaper. That's not the kind of pattern scientists are looking for, though! In science, a pattern is when data shows that one thing in your experiment is affected by something else.

Imagine you go out into your garden during the day and count how many open flowers you can find. You count 32. Once it gets dark you go out and count again. This time there are only ten open flowers. The next day, you do the same thing.

▼ These crocuses follow a pattern in nature. They are open during the day, and closed at night.

▲ Jane Goodall's observations changed what we know about chimpanzees. Here, she is recording data in a **journal**.

Once again, you find 32 open flowers during the day, but only ten open at night. The next day you do the same and get the same results.

Your data has a pattern. It shows that the time of day affects whether flowers are open or closed. This can also be called a **relationship** between the two things. Remember you should repeat your experiment to be sure of your results.

Awesome Observation

Famous **zoologist** Dr. Jane Goodall spent over 30 years living among wild chimpanzees. With only a pencil, a notebook, and binoculars, she made careful observations. These led to some amazing discoveries! People thought that chimpanzees were **vegetarians**, or animals that do not eat meat. But Goodall found out this wasn't true. She also observed chimpanzees making tools for gathering food like humans do.

GETTING IT RIGHT

The most important thing about recording data is honesty. Scientists must report data truthfully, even when it turns out differently than they expected. Changing data to fit a hypothesis means the experiment is of no use and the results are false. It's cheating!

▼ Imagine how dangerous it would be for this diabetic patient if her blood sugar test results were not reported correctly. Scientists who lie about results may harm people.

Dodgy Data

In the 1980s a scientist named Dr. Vijay R. Soman lied about his data. He was researching a disease called **diabetes**. His data didn't prove his hypothesis. Instead of reporting his data honestly, he lied. He made up data to prove his hypothesis. He even published his report in a **scientific journal**! He was caught cheating, and he lost his job. No one could trust what he said anymore. No one would hire him because he didn't behave honestly.

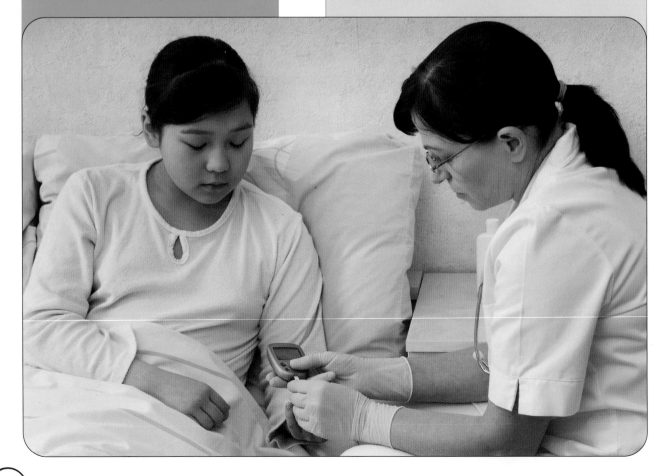

Hey, long time no see!

▲ This young scientist is collecting data about the eating habits of her goldfish. How do you think she will report her data?

Here are some of the different ways scientists record data:

You don't just have to be honest about your data. You also have to choose the right way to make and record your observations. Data can be collected and recorded in different ways. If you were observing the behavior of a goldfish, you might choose to record the data in words. But maybe you were collecting data about how many flakes of fish food the goldfish eats in one day. Then you might use a chart with numbers.

Numbers	Written Data and Pictures
table	journal
chart	diagram
computer software	video
	photograph
	drawings

MAKING OBSERVATIONS

Scientists are good observers. They record what they see, feel, hear, smell, and sometimes, taste.

Using the five senses is an important part of being a scientist. However, scientists must choose to use the right senses when they do their experiments. For example, they might be investigating the effect that "Silky Smooth Shampoo" has on the

▲ For this diver, the sense of sight is the right choice. She is choosing to look, and not touch!

softness of hair. If so, they wouldn't record observations about what the shampoo *smells* like! Also, scientists never taste, touch, or smell anything that is unsafe or unknown. They use the senses that make sense!

Look Closer

You might be amazed at how many observations you can make about very simple things. Take a pencil, for instance. Place it in your hand, and look at it closely. What do you notice? Try observing such things as weight, feel, color, length, and design. Record your observations on a piece of paper. Are you surprised at how many things you observed about a simple pencil?

▲ Food technicians use their sense of taste to test ingredients.

MEASURING MATTERS

Imagine that you and four other people are asked to build a house together. You are given the materials you need, and told to get started. However, everyone in the group speaks a different language. How would you begin when you can't even talk to everyone else?

In science, the way you measure things is very important. Many scientists use SI units, or Système international d'unités. That's French for International System of Units.

▶ The Golden Gate Bridge in San Francisco, California, was built by many engineers who worked together to achieve their goal.

SI units are **metric** units of measurement. These include units like centimeters, liters, and grams. Not every country uses metric units, however. Some countries use other units such as pounds, inches, and ounces. It is very important that when scientists record and report data, the unit of measurement is clear. This helps to avoid confusion or mistakes.

The Orbiter had a metric meltdown!

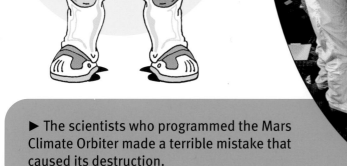

▶ The scientists who programmed the Mars Climate Orbiter made a terrible mistake that caused its destruction.

Lost in Space

Imagine destroying a spaceship! That's just what happened to NASA's Mars Climate Orbiter in 1999. A company called Lockheed Martin made some of the computer **equipment** for the Orbiter. However, they programmed the computer to use imperial units (e.g. inches) instead of metric units (e.g. centimeters). So, when NASA used metric units to steer the Orbiter toward Mars, it didn't do what they wanted. Because the units were not the same, the Orbiter burned up. Luckily there was no one aboard.

LET'S EXPERIMENT!

Dancing Raisins

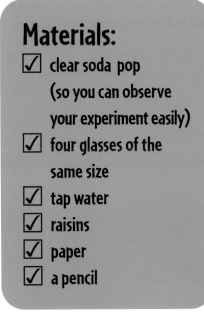

Materials:
- ☑ clear soda pop (so you can observe your experiment easily)
- ☑ four glasses of the same size
- ☑ tap water
- ☑ raisins
- ☑ paper
- ☑ a pencil

Problem

When did you last have a glass of soda pop? You may have noticed that there are many little bubbles in it. What do those bubbles do? They rise to the top, tickling your nose when you drink it! Those bubbles will even lift raisins. But how will a mix of soda pop and water change the way the raisins behave? Make a hypothesis and then do this experiment to find out.

1 Make a chart for recording your data. Use four rows **labeled** "Soda pop," "Half-soda pop, half-water," " Three-fourths water, one-fourth soda pop," and "Water." Beside each row, leave space. Here you can describe in words and pictures what you observe.

2 Fill one glass almost to the top with soda pop and set aside.

3 Next, fill a glass half full with soda pop, and add water for the other half. Leave a little room at the top of the glass.

4 Take the third glass, and fill it three-fourths of the way with water, and use soda pop to fill the rest of the way, almost to the top.

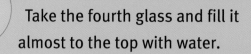

5 Take the fourth glass and fill it almost to the top with water.

6 Now add two raisins to each glass. Observe what happens. Record your data on your chart.

Take a Look!

What senses did you use to observe your experiment? What do you notice when you look at your data? Are there any patterns? Was your hypothesis correct?

NUMBER TALK

Tables, or charts, are useful for recording data that includes numbers. Scientists often use tables to organize their observations.

A table or chart is helpful for spotting patterns in data, or comparing information. They make information easy to understand at a glance. There are a few things to think about when you make a table or chart. Before you begin an experiment, you should think about the type of data you will be recording.

▼ This meteorologist is using an instrument called an *anemometer* to record wind speed during a hurricane. The data he gathers will be in numbers.

Science can blow you away!

Yes or No?

Numbers aren't the only information that can be recorded on a table or chart. Sometimes an experiment provides a "yes" or "no" answer to a question. For example, take the question "Which foods grow mold when left on the counter for one week?" The table would list the names of all the foods in your experiment. The table would also have a "yes" and a "no" column. You would mark the "yes" column or the "no" column depending on your results.

If your experiment includes taking measurements, decide which unit of measurement you will use. Include this information on your table—it's important! If you will be keeping a tally, make a simple tally chart beforehand.

▼ This girl is filling in the table with her data. Using the "yes" and "no" columns, she can clearly show which foods became moldy after one week.

PICTURE PERFECT

▲ One of the best ways to record data from outer space is through photographs. This photograph of the Horsehead Nebula was taken by the Hubble Telescope.

Sometimes, your results cannot be shown with numbers. Some data must be recorded in the form of photographs, drawings, or diagrams.

If you are taking a photograph, include a label for your photo. The label should describe what you're photographing, and when. For example, a label might read: "sample one: raisins in soda, no water, one minute after start of experiment."

Drawings should be as neat and accurate as possible. They can be useful for showing shapes and colors. For instance, if you needed to show how leaves changed in the fall, you could draw colored leaf shapes.

You can draw your own conclusions!

The Water Cycle

Have you ever seen a picture of how the water cycle works? It would probably look like this one. It shows exactly how water in the world moves and changes. It shows a lot of information very clearly. This is an example of a good diagram.

Diagrams are scientific pictures that have labels and a title. They need to be neat and detailed. A diagram is useful for showing how things work together, or the parts that make up a whole object. For instance, you could draw a diagram of the dancing raisins from the experiment on pages 14-15. Your diagram could include arrows showing how the raisins moved.

The Water Cycle

Sun

3. Up in the sky, the water vapor cools back into tiny liquid droplets that form clouds.

4. The droplets fall back to the ground as rain.

2. The water turns into water vapor, and rises into the air. This is called evaporation.

5. Rainwater flows into rivers, which carry it back to the sea.

1. Water in the oceans, rivers, and lakes gets heated by the Sun.

DIFFERENT DATA

In some experiments, sight is not very useful for making observations. Sometimes, scientists need to use hearing, touch, smell, or taste to make observations.

Imagine you are a scientist testing fire alarms. Your fire alarm has to make enough noise to wake the deepest sleeper in the middle of the night. You wouldn't find out which fire alarm was loudest just by looking at them! You would have to use your sense of hearing.

▶ Fire alarms can save lives during fires like this one. Scientists carefully test smoke alarms by using their sense of hearing to decide how loud alarms must be.

Sometimes, data can be difficult to record. You could try writing down a description of what something smelled or felt like. However, if you have a lot of data to record this could take a long time. In this case, you could try using symbols to show things. For example, if you were testing fire alarms, you could use a red circle to show the loudest alarm.

Listen Up!

Some scientists study patterns in the sounds made by whales. The best way to get whale sound data is by using special recording equipment. Today, scientists can **analyze** the data using a computer. In the past, they would have had to analyze their data using their ears!

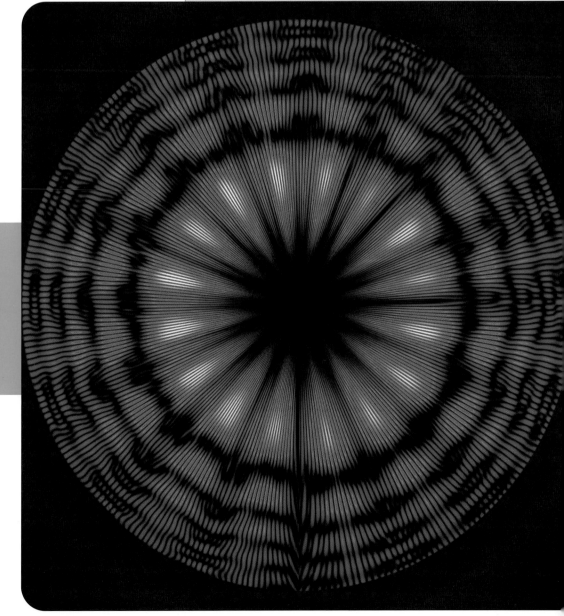

► This colorful picture shows the pattern of a humpback whale's song. Scientists use their sense of sight to read this data.

LET'S EXPERIMENT!

Rust Reasons

Materials:

- ☑ 5 small, empty, glass jars with tight-fitting lids (empty baby food jars work well)
- ☑ Tap water
- ☑ Cooking oil
- ☑ 1 teaspoon of salt
- ☑ Boiled water that has been slightly cooled (have an adult help you with boiling water)
- ☑ 5 small, clean, and dry steel nails (make sure they are not stainless or galvanized steel)

Problem

If you have ever been to an old, outdoor playground, you have probably seen rust on some of the metal equipment. What do you think causes this? In this experiment you are going to see what effect water, salt water, boiled water, cooking oil, and air have on steel. Make a hypothesis about what will happen.

1 Put one nail in each jar. Fill the first jar three-fourths full with tap water. Leave the jar open for now, and set it aside.

2 Next, fill another jar three-fourths of the way with cooking oil, and set aside.

3 Fill the third jar three-fourths full with a mixture of tap water and the salt. Stir to dissolve the salt. Set aside.

4 Do not put anything in the fourth jar—just leave it empty (apart from the nail).

5 Ask an adult to fill the fifth jar full with boiled water that has slightly cooled. Ask them to close the lid straightaway.

6 Now fasten the lids tightly on the other four jars. Leave the jars for one week, but look at them every day. What do you observe? Which nails rust first? Which ones rust the most? Are there any that don't rust at all? Be sure to record everything!

Take a Look!

Think about how you will record your data in this experiment. Could you use numbers, or would pictures be better? Would color drawings or photos be useful? Remember to observe carefully!

GETTING RESULTS

Sometimes experiments must be repeated over and over before an idea works out. Take Thomas Edison's light bulb experiments, for instance. He did invent a long-lasting light bulb, but guess how many tries it took? Over 700! He recorded the steps, materials, and results for each experiment. When his team of scientists became discouraged, he told them they hadn't failed. He said they had simply found 700 ways *not* to make a light bulb!

Edison never gave up on his bright idea!

▲ Thomas Edison made many attempts to create a long-lasting light bulb before he finally got it right.

When things go wrong, we learn from our mistakes. That's how we get closer to discovering the right way to do something.

Rocket Science

There have been many experiments that turned out differently than expected. One was the Vanguard rocket launch in 1957. The rocket was unmanned, which means there were no people aboard. This was lucky, because during the launch, the rocket burst into flames! It was all over in less than two seconds. Yet the launch was not a total failure. The rocket had sent a small amount of data before it burned up. Even though their experiment didn't work the way they hoped, the scientists made the best of the situation.

◄ Even though it exploded during its launch, the Vanguard rocket gave scientists some important data.

WHAT NOW?

Once you've collected your data, the next step is to carefully read it. This is where scientists look for what their data shows. This is called analyzing.

Question Time

Here is a list of some useful questions. Scientists ask themselves these questions when they look closely at their results. It helps them figure out what the data is telling them:

- Did I make sure that the data was recorded correctly?

- When I look at the data, do I see any patterns?

- How can the experiment be made better?

- What could be done differently?

- Have I got any new questions from the experiment or data?

▶ There is always more to learn about our Earth, and other worlds, too.

▲ We make discoveries about the world by asking questions. If we go on asking, we will never stop learning!

To make sure that data is honestly reported, there are some rules for scientists. They must keep careful, detailed notes about every step of an experiment. When they have a new discovery or invention to share, they write a report. Then they have to send their report to other scientists to be checked for mistakes. This way, errors are usually found early on.

Finally, the report is published in a scientific journal for everyone to read. This process helps other scientists to find out if a scientist has made a mistake or, worse, is telling lies. It helps keep science honest and useful.

KEEPING A JOURNAL

Parents often record data about their new baby. They might write down weight, length, hair color, eye color, and personality traits. They take a lot of pictures and write down favorite memories in a special book. Some parents also record what their baby does using a video camera.

Scientists record their observations in much the same way as parents. A journal is one of the best ways to record information.

A journal can be anything from a scrapbook, to a binder with lined paper, from a computer file, to a notepad. The important thing about a journal is that it is where scientists record everything about their experiment, from beginning to end.

▼ This young scientist is carefully recording his observations in a journal.

In this step, you can use a journal to record your data. Tables, written observations, diagrams, notes on recordings, photos, drawings, and symbols can all be part of a journal. Gathering the data in a journal is a great way to make sure you have recorded all of your observations.

Here are some tips for keeping your journal:

- Make sure you write the date every time you use your journal;

- Have your journal with you every time you observe your experiment. Otherwise, you might forget observations before you have the chance to write them down;

- Be clear and specific. Label drawings and diagrams, and don't forget to record units of measurement;

- Include your observations and data in detail.

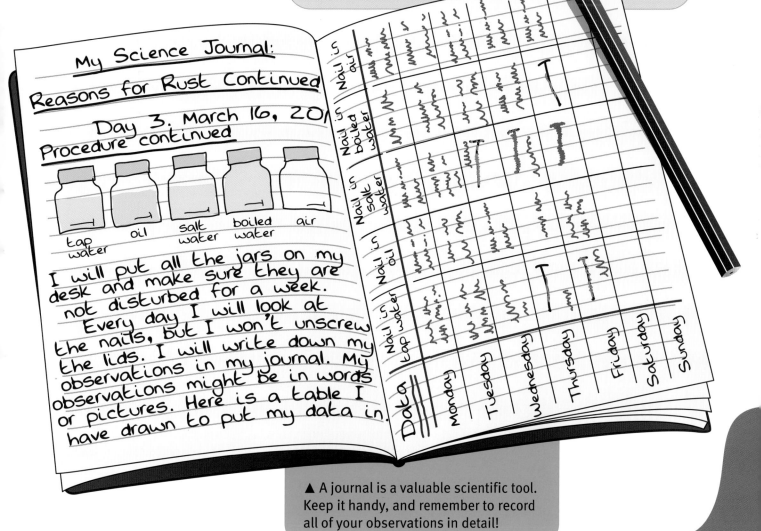

My Science Journal:
Reasons for Rust Continued
Day 3, March 16, 20
Procedure continued

tap water   oil   salt water   boiled water   air

I will put all the jars on my desk and make sure they are not disturbed for a week. Every day I will look at the nails, but I won't unscrew the lids. I will write down my observations in my journal. My observations might be in words or pictures. Here is a table I have drawn to put my data in.

▲ A journal is a valuable scientific tool. Keep it handy, and remember to record all of your observations in detail!

TIMELINE

Below is a list of scientific discoveries and inventions that were the result of careful data collection.

Year	Discovery or invention	Who collected the data that led to the discovery or invention?
1522	Around the world by boat	The crew of Magellan's ship *Victoria* are the first people to go all the way around the world. They record data about the Pacific Ocean that is used to make maps.
1796	Smallpox vaccine	Edward Jenner makes carefully written observations. These lead to the development of a breakthrough vaccine to treat smallpox.
1822	The first dinosaur fossil	Geologist William Buckland finds a dinosaur fossil in England. In his journal he records data about the size, shape, age, color, and location of the fossil.
1827	The first photograph	Joseph Nicéphore Niépce invents the camera. This is the first time information is recorded as a photograph.
1838	The theory of cells	Matthias Schleiden uses a microscope to study plants. He identifies and makes diagrams of the many small cells that all plants contain.
1960s	Chimpanzees are observed making tools	Jane Goodall observes a chimp making a tool for getting termites. Before this, everyone thought humans were the only ones to make tools.
1999	Tagging of Pacific Predators Program	The Census of Marine Life records data about the movement of sharks using satellite tracking and sound sensors.

GLOSSARY

analyze To study information to find out what it means

chart A way of showing numbers in rows and columns. Also called a table

data Scientific information

diabetes A quite common condition that affects how the body gets its energy

equipment The physical things needed for something

galvanized steel Steel which has been coated in zinc to stop it rusting

graph A diagram that can illustrate the results of an experiment. A graph has one measurement along the bottom, and another up the side

hypothesis An educated guess about what your experiment will prove

journal A record of every step of an experiment

label Words explaining parts of an image

metric A system of measurement used by most scientists

observations Noticing something happening by using the five senses

pattern When data shows a connection between one thing and another

relationship How one thing affects another thing

research Finding out facts about something

results The information that comes from an experiment

scientific journal A magazine that publishes important scientific discoveries

scientific method The way to do an experiment properly

stainless steel A type of steel that does not stain or rust as easily as regular steel

table Organized columns and rows for showing information. It is also called a chart

vegetarians Animals, including humans, which don't eat meat

zoologist A scientist who studies animals

FURTHER INFORMATION

Books

My Big Science Book, Roger Priddy, Priddy Books, January 2004

One Minute Mysteries: 65 Short Mysteries You Solve With Science!, Eric Yoder, Science Naturally, September 2008

Web sites

www.brainpopjr.com/science/

www.funology.com/laboratory/

INDEX

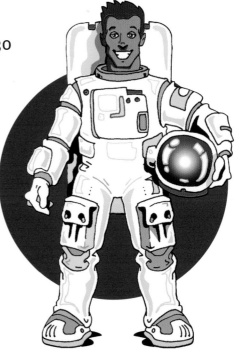